Acting Edition

VEINS AND THUMBTACKS

BY JONATHAN MARC SHERMAN

DPS
DRAMATISTS PLAY SERVICE

For Jay's magical spirit.

VEINS AND THUMBTACKS received its world premiere at the Los Angeles Theatre Center (Bill Bushnell, Artistic Director; Diane White, Producing Director), in Los Angeles, California, on February 7, 1991. It was directed by David Saint; the set design was by David Gallo; the costume design was by Marianna Elliott; the lighting design was by Kenneth Posner; the sound design was by Jon Gottlieb and the stage manager was Nancy Ann Adler. The cast was as follows:

ANNIE ....Elizabeth Berridge
ARTURO CONSTANTINI ....Bruce MacVittie
GRANDMOTHER ....Beatrice Manley
CHAPEL OWNER, DIVORCE GUY,
      CALLER ....William Marquez
WENDY BONAPARTE ....Mercedes McNab
NURSE, TRALICE..Noelle Parker
JIMMY BONAPARTE ....Fisher Stevens

CHARACTERS

Jimmy Bonaparte
Grandmother
Annie
Owner of the Neon Bells Wedding Chapel
Nurse
Arturo Constantini
Divorce Guy
Tralice
Caller
Wendy Bonaparte

TIME

1978 to 1989.

NOTE

The spirit of New Jersey should loom underneath the play so the characters know where they stand.

"Ice cream
Runs through my veins." – James Oswald Bonaparte

VEINS AND
THUMBTACKS

Scene One

The den. Jimmy is standing. Grandmother is in her wheel-chair.

JIMMY.   I'm gonna take an *axe*, Grandma, I'm gonna chop into your *neck*. I'm gonna chop till your head falls off, and I'm gonna reach into your neck and start pulling out the *veins*, one by one, I'm gonna pull out the veins from your *wrinkle* of a neck, I'm gonna get some *thumbtacks*, and I'm gonna tack your veins to the *walls*. I'm gonna fill the walls up with your dripping veins.
GRANDMOTHER.   *Fuck* you, Jimmy.
JIMMY.   Fuck *me?* Fuck *you*. Alright? Fuck *you*. Put on your bifocals and read my lips: *Fuck You.*
GRANDMOTHER.   Big man. Big *talker*.
JIMMY.   Keep trying to get me going. Just keep it up. I'm gonna crack your bifocals and make you eat the glass before I chop off your head. That way, the veins will be *bite* size, 'cause the glass'll tear 'em all apart. Veins as long as my thumb, and I'm gonna tack 'em to the walls about an inch apart from each other, and I'm going to laugh my head off.
GRANDMOTHER.   You'll laugh your head off and it'll roll to the floor next to mine, is that the idea?
JIMMY.   Don't get wise. Don't be getting *smart*.
GRANDMOTHER.   You the only *genius* allowed in the family, is that it? Always *talking*. Always *babbling*.
JIMMY.   I'm gonna chop up your brain, put it in the blender, add some lemons, and make some *lemonade*. You hear me?

GRANDMOTHER.   I wish I *didn't* hear you. You give me a *headache*. All of your *plans*. All your *schemes*. A million *schemes*. I've never seen *one* of them.
JIMMY.   Keep quiet. Keep *shut*.
GRANDMOTHER.   You *talk*. I've never seen you *do*.
JIMMY.   I wonder fucking *why* you've never seen me do. Look in the mirror, if it doesn't crack from your *ugliness*.
GRANDMOTHER.   *Ugly?* You —
JIMMY.   *You. You* are the ugliness. *You* are the reason I can't *do* anything. You go on, saying *this*, telling me why don't I *do*. It's *you. You're* the reason. I could have built the biggest mountain in the *country* by now if it wasn't for you.
GRANDMOTHER.   You couldn't build a damn *thing*.
JIMMY.   I *could*. I could *too*. Without you to deal with, I could do anything I wanted. Don't you *get* it? Don't you *see?* You're ruining my youth. I'm *young*. I'm supposed to *enjoy* it. I'm supposed to have a good time. I *want* to have a good time. Hell, I'm *virile*. I'm the goddamn American *Dream*. But instead of *doing* stuff, I gotta work at the goddamn supermarket, and then I gotta come home and take *care* of you. You and your *medication*. I don't give a shit about you, you know that?
GRANDMOTHER.   I don't give a shit about *you*, you *ingrate*.
JIMMY.   You dying sack of *bones*. You grey *lump*. If I didn't have to tend to you after school, do you know what my life would be *like?* Do you know what I'd be *doing? Hah?* Do you? *Do* you?
GRANDMOTHER.   *(Pause.)* Probably *talking*, knowing you.
JIMMY.   *Shut up.*
GRANDMOTHER.   If your parents could see you now —
JIMMY.   I said shut up, I *said* it, I *meant* it. Shut up. Just keep quiet. I want *silence. (Pause.)* You know, Grandma —
ANNIE.   *(Off.) Jimmy?*
JIMMY.   *(Pause.)* Yeah, in here. *(Annie walks in.)*
ANNIE.   Jimmy. I was ringing the bell —
JIMMY.   Yeah, it's *broke*.
ANNIE.   It *is?*
JIMMY.   *Today*. It just broke *today*.

ANNIE.   Oh. Hello, Mrs. Bonaparte.
GRANDMOTHER.   Hello.
ANNIE.   How are you doing today?
GRANDMOTHER.   Well, Jimmy's all mad and yelling —
JIMMY.   She's doing *fine.* What's up?
ANNIE.   I got to *talk* to you. I got something to *tell* you.
JIMMY.   Yeah? What is it?
ANNIE.   It's kind of *important.*
JIMMY.   So *tell* me.
ANNIE.   I mean, it's kind of *private.* No offense, Mrs. Bonaparte —
JIMMY.   It don't matter, you can say it in front of the old bag of *shit* —
ANNIE.   *Jimmy* —
JIMMY.   It doesn't matter *what* she hears, 'cause I'm going to cut off her fucking ears and throw them in the trash barrel in a couple of minutes.
GRANDMOTHER.   Bullshit, Jimmy. Just like you, Jimmy. Bullshit.
JIMMY.   I *mean* it.
GRANDMOTHER.   You always *say* you mean it, you never *mean* it.
JIMMY.   You want I should do it *right* now, *right* here? *Huh?*
ANNIE.   Jimmy, cut it out.
JIMMY.   *(Pause.)* You are *lucky* Annie showed up when she did, Grandma, just remember that. Just *know* that.
GRANDMOTHER.   I'll bet.
JIMMY.   *(To Annie.)* So, what is it?
ANNIE.   I'm pregnant.
JIMMY.   *(Pause.)* What's that mean?
ANNIE.   It means I'm going to have a baby come out of me. *Pregnant.*
JIMMY.   *(Pause.)* Oh, shit. *(Jimmy covers his hand with his mouth. To Grandmother.)* I'll deal with you later. Go in the kitchen.
GRANDMOTHER.   You don't order me —
JIMMY.   *(Screaming.)* Go in the kitchen, Grandma! Go in the kitchen, Grandma! *Right now! (Grandmother wheels herself out.)*

And don't you touch my beer, you hear me? If I go in there and you touched my beer, I'm gonna take the wheels off your chair! *(To Annie.)* She takes my beer out of the refrigerator and empties it down the drain, I tell you that? Like I don't work my ass off hard enough to have to deal with *that.* You *believe* that? Sometimes —
ANNIE.   Jimmy, I'm pregnant.
JIMMY.   I heard you the first time.
ANNIE.   So if you heard me the first time, what are you doing talking about *beer?* I'm *pregnant.* I don't *care* about your beer.
JIMMY.   You and Grandma both.
ANNIE.   *Jimmy* —
JIMMY.   Okay, Okay. *(Pause.)* So what are we gonna do?
ANNIE.   I don't know, Jimmy. *(Pause.)* I don't know. *(Pause.)* I'm *scared* —
JIMMY.   Hey. *Hey.* Look who's here. *I'm* here. Nothing to be scared about. Things are gonna be okay. We'll get an *abortion* —
ANNIE.   I *can't.*
JIMMY.   *Huh?*
ANNIE.   You *know* I can't.
JIMMY.   I *do?* I do *not.* Why *can't* you?
ANNIE.   Come on, Jimmy. I'm a *Catholic.* You know that. I can't get an abortion.
JIMMY.   What you think God's got so much free time that he's going to make a big deal out of you getting a *baby* aborted?
ANNIE.   I can't do it. You *know* that. It's not an option.
JIMMY.   Yes, it is. It's a *good* option. Don't say it's *not* an option.
ANNIE.   It is not an option.
JIMMY.   When the hell did you get so goddamn *religious,* huh? Tell me that. If you're so damn Catholic, why were you dating me? Huh? I'm not Catholic. I'm *Jewish.* How come you're going out with a Jew if you're so Catholic? You guys think we killed Jesus, for Chrissakes.
ANNIE.   Jimmy, I go out with you because I *like* you.

JIMMY.   Yeah, well, a *real* Catholic *wouldn't* like me, right, 'cause I'm not a Catholic. So that means you're not *real.* You're not a strict Catholic. A strict Catholic would never *get* pregnant, because a strict Catholic would never have *sex.* Not until they got *married,* at least, and then only once in a while.
ANNIE.   It's not just being Catholic, Jimmy, it's a *belief.* A way of *thinking.* I can't *kill* a person, especially my own *child.*
JIMMY.   It's not a person yet. It's not your child yet. It's about as big as a *pencil* point. It doesn't even know a *thing* yet. *(Pause.)* Hey, how do you even know you're pregnant? Tell me *that.*
ANNIE.   I didn't — I wasn't getting my period, I took a test, I *know.*
JIMMY.   Yeah, but tests —
ANNIE.   I *know.*
JIMMY.   *(Pause.)* Why can you date me and do it with me and that's okay, but when it comes to getting an abortion, which would make things much easier, why can't you do that?
ANNIE.   I *can't. (Pause.)* And I *won't.*
JIMMY.   *(Pause.) Fine. Be* that way. *Think* that way. *(Pause.)* What about getting it adopted?
ANNIE.   Jimmy, my parents are going to *kill* me. They — I — Jimmy —
JIMMY.   Annie —
ANNIE.   I'm really scared.
JIMMY.   Yeah, okay, but that doesn't get anything *done.* That doesn't *help* anything. All it does is it makes me *nervous.* We've got to *do* something. What are we gonna *do* about this thing?
ANNIE.   *(Pause.)* We could get married.
JIMMY.   *Married?* Annie, I'm *eighteen,* I'm still in *high* school, I haven't even *graduated* yet, you think I want to get *married?*
ANNIE.   You think I do, either? You think I want to be *preg-nant?* I don't *want* this, I didn't *plan* this, this just *happened.* We *made* it happen. And *we* have to figure it out. And if we have to get married, then we *have* to.
JIMMY.   Oh, *fuck. (Pause.)* I ain't getting you a wedding ring.

Scene Two

The Neon Bells Wedding Chapel. Jimmy and Annie are standing before the Owner.

OWNER.   And do you, James Oswald Bonaparte, take this woman to be your lawfully wedded wife?
JIMMY.   Yeah, I do.
OWNER.   I now pronounce you man and wife. You may kiss the bride. *(Pause.)* I said you may kiss the bride.
JIMMY.   I don't feel like it right now, okay?
OWNER.   Uhh, no, it's not okay. It's the policy of the Neon Bells Wedding Chapel that every man must kiss every wife.
JIMMY.   But I don't really want to.
OWNER.   I'm sorry, but you must. I insist.
JIMMY.   *Why?*
OWNER.   It's tradition. I can't very well marry two people with all my heart when they don't even want to *kiss* one another, can I?
JIMMY.   I've kissed her before, lots of times.
OWNER.   Well, you've got to do it in front of me.
JIMMY.   This is stupid. This is *really* stupid.
ANNIE.   Jimmy.
JIMMY.   What?
ANNIE.   Give me your lips. *(Annie kisses Jimmy.)* There. How's that?
OWNER.   Uhh, I guess that's okay. I mean, that was just fine, but technically the man's supposed to kiss the bride.
ANNIE.   It was a *mutual* kiss.
JIMMY.   You said I *may* kiss the bride, not I *have* to. Now cut the shit. Are we married or not?
OWNER.   Uhh, yes, yes, I guess you are.
JIMMY.   Let's go.
OWNER.   Wait. You get a Polaroid. It comes with the package.
JIMMY.   I don't want a frigging *Polaroid.*
ANNIE.   Jimmy, cut it out. Take the Polaroid, please. *(Owner*

photographs Jimmy and Annie with a Polaroid camera.)
OWNER.   Just got to wait sixty seconds for it to develop.
JIMMY.   Oh, *Jesus.*
OWNER.   *(Pause.)* Where you folks from?
ANNIE.   New Jersey.
OWNER.   Nice up in Jersey. I was there a few years back. My brother moved there. You come down to Vegas just to have a wedding?
ANNIE.   Jimmy wanted to. He wanted to see what Vegas was like.
OWNER.   Lots of people come down here to get married.
JIMMY.   Is the picture done?
OWNER.   Not just yet, nope.
JIMMY.   *(Pause.)* Why is that?
OWNER.   Why's *what?*
JIMMY.   Why is it people come down to Las Vegas to get married so much? Why is that, you figure?
OWNER.   I don't know for sure. I would guess it's the festive, fun atmosphere around here. It's like a party that never quits.
JIMMY.   Yeah.
OWNER.   Also, lot of people come in here drunk as hell.
JIMMY.   That makes sense. It's probably easier to take when you're drunk.
ANNIE.   Stop that, Jimmy.
JIMMY.   I bet it is. Everything's a blur, you say "I do," kiss a little and toss your life down the toilet. Along with all your money.
OWNER.   Picture's developed. *(Owner hands the photograph to Annie.)*
ANNIE.   Aww, that came out nice.
JIMMY.   I look like *shit.*
ANNIE.   Will you *stop?* Thank you very much, sir. You have a lovely chapel.
OWNER.   I like to think it's the loveliest chapel in Nevada.
ANNIE.   Thanks again. Take care now.
OWNER.   Bye.
JIMMY.   You should get a shotgun in this place, you know,

for shotgun weddings. I feel like shooting myself in the skull.
OWNER.   Ha, ha. That's very funny, James. *(Annie and Jimmy walk out.)* You have a wonderful life, now, you hear? Bye.

Scene Three

Annie's hospital room. Annie is in bed. Jimmy walks in, holding a bunch of flowers.

JIMMY.   Hey.
ANNIE.   Hey.
JIMMY.   How you feeling?
ANNIE.   Okay.
JIMMY.   Where's the baby?
ANNIE.   The nurse just went to go get her.
JIMMY.   She's gonna bring it in?
ANNIE.   Yeah.
JIMMY.   Into the room?
ANNIE.   Yeah. What'd you think?
JIMMY.   I don't know. I always thought you had to see it through glass or something.
ANNIE.   No, she's going to bring her in here.
JIMMY.   Oh. *(Pause.)* I got you some flowers.
ANNIE.   Thanks.
JIMMY.   You're welcome. I was thinking maybe some chocolates or something, but I figured you'll be trying to lose some weight now that the baby's out of you, so I got flowers.
ANNIE.   They're nice.
JIMMY.   Thanks. Should I just put them over here?
ANNIE.   Yeah, I don't have a vase or anything. Maybe the nurse will bring me one, after she brings in the baby.
JIMMY.   I can't wait. You know, I'm *nervous.*
ANNIE.   Really?
JIMMY.   Yeah. Go figure. Hey, we have to name it now, right?
ANNIE.   I guess we do.

JIMMY.   I was kind of hoping to name it Steve, but I guess that's no good now, huh?
ANNIE.   I don't like Steve for a girl. How about Stephanie?
JIMMY.   No, Stephanie sounds like you're trying to prove something. I never met a Stephanie I really *related* to, you know?
ANNIE.   I guess so. How about Heather? I always liked Heather.
JIMMY.   Sounds like somebody who grew up on a farm.
ANNIE.   Heather sounds like somebody who grew up on a farm?
JIMMY.   To me it does.
ANNIE.   What about Emily?
JIMMY.   Emily sucks.
ANNIE.   It's my *mother's* name.
JIMMY.   I know.
ANNIE.   Why do you have to be so mean? Huh? All the time, you're so mean.
JIMMY.   I just don't like the name Emily. I want my girl to have a name that I like to *say*. Is that so bad?
ANNIE.   So what's a name you like to say?
JIMMY.   I don't know. What about Wendy?
ANNIE.   *Wendy?* Are you serious?
JIMMY.   Yeah, Wendy. Like *Peter Pan*. She took care of the Lost Boys, right?
ANNIE.   Oh, *Jimmy*.
JIMMY.   *What?*
ANNIE.   What, like, you're a Lost Boy and she's going to take care of you, is that what you're saying?
JIMMY.   Where the fuck did you get that from? I just liked that Wendy did that in the story. Is that a crime?
ANNIE.   What's Wendy Diesel going to think?
JIMMY.   Huh? What are you bringing up her for?
ANNIE.   What am *I* bringing up her for? Your ex-girlfriend is named Wendy and you want to name our child Wendy and you're asking me what *I'm* bringing it up for?
JIMMY.   Wendy Diesel has nothing to do with me wanting to name the baby Wendy. That is so *stupid.*

ANNIE.   So is Wendy Diesel.

JIMMY.   Oh, that's precious. If I didn't break up with her, I'd be better off than I am now.

ANNIE.   You didn't break up with her, she broke up with you. In the cafeteria. I was there, remember?

JIMMY.   Look, there are two different names we are talking about here. There is the kind of Wendy that is Wendy Diesel, and then there is the *Peter Pan* Wendy, which I brought up. They are two completely different things.

ANNIE.   Spelled exactly the same way.

JIMMY.   That's right.

ANNIE.   Well, if there can be two different Wendys, there can be two different Heathers. The one that grew up on a farm and the one that's a name that I like.

JIMMY.   See, you're not making sense now. Now, you're just arguing to *argue*. I'm going to give you a choice. We can name the child Wendy — not in reference to Wendy Diesel, but in reference to *Peter Pan* — and everything will be fine. *Or* we can name the child *Heather*, which sounds like somebody who should milk *cows*, in which case I will *still* call the kid Wendy, and the kid will be very confused, and probably grow up to be crazy and live in an institution as a schizophrenic. *You* decide. (*A Nurse walks in, holding a baby.*)

NURSE.   Mr. and Mrs. Bonaparte, here's your little girl. (*The Nurse brings the baby over to Annie. Jimmy walks over.*)

JIMMY.   (*Pause.*) She's the most beautiful thing I have ever seen.

ANNIE.   Isn't she — what's that smell?

NURSE.   Is it the baby?

ANNIE.   Jimmy, have you been drinking?

JIMMY.   What? So what?

ANNIE.   You're *drunk*. I can't believe you're *drunk* the first time you see our daughter.

JIMMY.   Big deal. I drank some beers. I'm fine.

ANNIE.   You can't just do something *regular*, can you? You always have to figure out a way to mess things up. Nothing can be right or happy or good, because that makes you *nervous*.

JIMMY.   Will you be quiet and let me see my daughter? *(Pause.)* She's got my eyes.
ANNIE.   She's got *my* eyes. She's got your *mouth.*
JIMMY.   Thank God she doesn't have *yours. (Pause.)* She's *terrific. (To Nurse.)* Hey, what do you think of the name Wendy for this baby?
NURSE.   It's a lovely name.
JIMMY.   See, Annie, it's a *lovely* name. Even the nurse thinks so. Nobody even thinks of Wendy Diesel.
ANNIE.   Nobody but me, right?
JIMMY.   If you would just *forget* about that and listen to the way it sounds and look at the baby at the same time, you'd know it was *right. (Pause.) Wendy. (Pause.)* Look, she sort of smiled, even. She *loves* it. It's meant to be. She's a Wendy if ever I've seen one.
ANNIE.   Let's see if you still like it when you're *sober.*
JIMMY.   Will you cut the *shit? Alright?* Just cut the *shit.* You always give me crap about stuff that's just *crap.*
ANNIE.   I —
JIMMY.   Will you look at that wonderful baby?
ANNIE.   I — Jimmy, if it's going to make you happy, Wendy is a fine name.
JIMMY.   You *mean* it?
ANNIE.   But her middle name is *Heather.*
JIMMY.   If her *middle* name wants to milk cows, I could care less. Middle names are about as important as substitute teachers.
ANNIE.   I just don't want to fight all the time. It wears me out. I want stuff to go right, you know?
JIMMY.   I know. Oh, I know. You'll see. Wendy'll make things *good.* It's going to be good. Just look at our *kid.* Look at beautiful little *Wendy.*
ANNIE.   Beautiful little — *Wendy (Pause.)* She is beautiful, isn't she, Jimmy?
JIMMY.   You better believe it. She's the most beautiful beauty ... of all the beauties. *(Pause.)* Hey, Annie, I've been thinking about religion.
ANNIE.   *You?*

JIMMY. I mean, for the *kid,* you know? And on the way over here, in the car, I figured it out.
ANNIE. And?
JIMMY. *And,* she'll be Catholic for four days a week and she can be Jewish the other three days. I gave you the extra day on account of you care more about the issue than I do. I figure Jewish on Sunday, Monday and Tuesday, Catholic on Wednesday through Saturday. That way, on Sunday, she won't be Catholic and on Saturday, she won't be Jewish, so she won't have to go to services for either religion and she can do whatever she wants.
ANNIE. Jimmy, you're drunk.
JIMMY. Maybe, but it's still a good idea. Don't let the alcohol get in your way. It's a great idea.
ANNIE. It doesn't make sense. Nobody's going to buy it. You can't be a part-time Catholic.
JIMMY. You sort of were.
ANNIE. What are you *talking* about?
JIMMY. Well, when we were having sex — *(To Nurse.)* pardon me, Miss.
NURSE. That's okay. I'm a nurse.
JIMMY. Right. *(To Annie.)* You weren't Catholic when we would have sex, because a Catholic wouldn't *have* sex, especially not with a Jew. But you *were* Catholic when you'd go to mass, and you were *definitely* Catholic when you got pregnant.
ANNIE. Jimmy, I was Catholic the whole time, even when we had sex. I was still Catholic, I was just a *bad* Catholic.
JIMMY. And you were *bad.* And I mean *bad.*
ANNIE. Jimmy —
JIMMY. What? *(Annie indicates that the Nurse is in the room and she's embarrassed.)* She's a nurse, she doesn't mind. *(To Nurse.)* Do you?
NURSE. Not at all.
JIMMY. See?
NURSE. Mr. Bonaparte, did you say you're *Jewish?*
JIMMY. Yeah. Why? What's wrong?
NURSE. Oh, nothing, but with a name like *Bonaparte* —
JIMMY. Yeah, I know. My ancestors and all came over to

America with a big old Russian Jewish name and changed it to Bonaparte, which they thought sounded American.
NURSE.   I see.
JIMMY.   We have a tough time with names in my family.
NURSE.   I understand.
JIMMY.   We have a tough time *period* in my family. But now I got a *daughter.* And things are looking *up.*
ANNIE.   Jimmy, don't forget, she isn't *just* beautiful, she's a *baby,* a *responsibility.*
JIMMY.   I know, I know. But she's *beautiful.*
NURSE.   I should take her back now.
JIMMY.   One second. I just need one good long look. *(Long pause.)* Okay. You can take her back now. Be careful with her.
NURSE.   I will be. *(The Nurse takes the baby and walks out.)*
JIMMY.   She's so *beautiful.* I just — I can't get over it. *(Pause.)* I have a *daughter!*
ANNIE.   What a coincidence. So do I. *(Jimmy kisses Annie.)* You taste like *beer.*
JIMMY.   *Deal* with it.

Scene Four

The Laugh Riot's stage. Jimmy walks on and picks up a microphone.

JIMMY.   Pleasure to be here at the Laugh Riot's bi-weekly amateur night. I'm Jimmy Bonaparte, and ice cream runs through my veins. My sixth grade teacher told me that and I've never been able to forget it, especially since every time I get a paper cut, something pink that tastes like strawberry comes out instead of blood. I don't know. Anyhow, this is my first time up here at the Laugh Riot, and I'm pretty psyched, especially for you guys, because it's going to be a pleasure to spend five minutes with me, let me tell you in advance. I'm one of the most interesting people I know. Of course, you should see the people I know. No, I'm just kidding. I just had a baby girl, she's six months old. Thank you. I knew she was a girl when the nurse showed her to me and I looked down and there was no *dick*. I thought to myself, this is a girl. My wife and I always do it in the dark, and why the hell not, right? What do I want to look at me trying hard and sweating and blasting inside her and all of that for? With the lights off, I imagine I look like Clark Gable. And *she* looks like Clark Gable. In fact, once the lights go off, everybody looks like Clark Gable to me, I can't figure it out. Clark Gable. "Frankly, Scarlett, I don't *give* a damn." I said that to my friend Arturo who works with me in the supermarket. I turned to him the other day out of the blue and says, "Frankly, Arturo, I don't *give* a damn." He said, "Shut up and keep putting the prices on the soup cans." He's a great guy. Arturo Constantini's his name. He was going to come tonight, but his girlfriend stood him up, so he decided to watch TV instead. Very interesting people you meet at the supermarket. And the thing is, you think about all of the people in there that shop while you work, because your work is so *boring*. And you think dirty thoughts about these people. These innocent people, just buying cucumbers, and I think we all know *why* women buy cucumbers. To make salads, that's right, *sure* it is. This one lady comes in all the time, she's a blonde, and I have this daydream about her, that I write these love notes with a Magic Marker on the inside of her vagina and she's screaming, full of discomfort, begging me to stop, but I just keep writing these love notes on her vagina. And it's a *special* vagina, you see, because it plays tapes. *Eight* tracks. God, what the hell *is* a vagina, anyhow? Speaking of *vaginas*, my wife is a ballbreaker. She won't do anything to make me happy. Even when she gave me blue balls, they were *turquoise*. She's a real tough cookie. She's *Catholic*, you see. She went on this camping trip with her church once, I said, "What about *bears*? Do you have a *bear* trap?" She said, "My *vagina* is a bear trap." Ever since then, I act *real* nice to her. Except tonight. Tonight, while she was taking a nap, I rubbed Crazy Glue all over her cleavage so her tits'll stick together. Speaking of sticky tits — ahh, forget it. I don't like that. You know, it's funny, I get nostalgic ever since I graduated from high school, ever since I was released into this living hell they call the Real World. I miss high school. I dated this girl in high school who shot darts out of her vagina, and it could also shuffle a deck of cards. Compared to that, my wife's bear trap just seems tame. Anyway, thanks, you've been great, and if you think my act was disgusting, just look at your lives. I'm Jimmy Bonaparte. Young, Fresh, Angry. Thanks a lot. *(Jimmy drops the microphone and walks off.)*

Scene Five

The supermarket. Jimmy and Arturo are putting price stickers on cans.

JIMMY.   I was sweating like crazy, right, but on the *inside*. It was the weirdest thing.
ARTURO.   You were sweating on the inside?
JIMMY.   Yeah.
ARTURO.   That *is* weird.
JIMMY.   But it was a high. A *definite* rush.
ARTURO.   Sounds good.
JIMMY.   It *was* good. And I think I'm *good* at it. I mean, I can't really tell what people thought, but fuck them if they don't like it. I can still be *good*. What the hell do *they* know?
ARTURO.   Are you going to do it again?
JIMMY.   I think so. Yeah. Definitely. I figure if I keep doing it long enough, I can get better and better and maybe eventually I'll be *great*, you know?
ARTURO.   Sure.
JIMMY.   I mean, something like comedy takes a lot of practice, I mean, to get to where you can be professional at it.
ARTURO.   Yeah, it must take a long time.
JIMMY.   Sure. And, you know, I've got a lot of other stuff brewing as well. I'll tell you one thing, I am *not* just a guy who works in a supermarket.
ARTURO.   Good for you.
JIMMY.   Yeah. *(Pause.)* How long you think you'll work here?

ARTURO.   I don't know. A while, maybe. I don't mind it,
really. I like this place. I worked over at the Pathmark for a
while, and the people just weren't friendly at all, but the
people here are pretty nice to me, and I don't mind it.
JIMMY.   Yeah, I know, but it just gets to me all the time, af-
ter a while, I mean. Fucking *produce,* and *cereal,* and *milk,* you
know?
ARTURO.   The cereal aisle's a little bright, don't you think?
JIMMY.   Bright?
ARTURO.   I mean, all those different colors. It isn't a very
calm place.
JIMMY.   Yeah, and there's always kids in there.
ARTURO.   Yeah.
JIMMY.   I mean, I like kids, but kids in a supermarket are
brats.
ARTURO.   They do make a lot of *noise.*
JIMMY.   Fucking love to run them over with a *cart* or some-
thing.
ARTURO.   Hey, how's your daughter doing?
JIMMY.   Wendy? She's good, she's real good. *Adorable,* you
know.
ARTURO.   That's good.
JIMMY.   *(Pause.)* Hey, Arturo, see that lady in the fur coat?
ARTURO.   Yeah?
JIMMY.   Think she's got anything on underneath it?
ARTURO.   *(Pause.)* Yeah, she probably does.
JIMMY.   Yeah, you're probably right.

Scene Six

*The den. Annie is sitting on the couch, wrapped in a blan-
ket, watching television. The room is dark.*

JIMMY.   *(Off.)* Annie!
ANNIE.   *(Trying to keep quiet.)* In here! *(Jimmy walks in.)*
JIMMY.   I was scared to death —

ANNIE.   Quiet, you'll wake up Wendy. Come sit down.
JIMMY.   *(Sitting.)* I was scared to death —
ANNIE.   What happened?
JIMMY.   I was having the worst nightmare, fucking unbelieva-
bly horrible, and I woke up and I was all alone.
ANNIE.   I couldn't sleep.
JIMMY.   I didn't know where you were.
ANNIE.   I'm right here. What were you dreaming about?
JIMMY.   I was little.
ANNIE.   What? You were a little boy again?
JIMMY.   I was little. And then when I woke up and you
weren't there, I didn't know where you were, and you
weren't there.
ANNIE.   I'm right here, Jimmy. I'm here. *(Annie holds Jimmy.
He looks like a small child, curled up in her arms. Beat.)* Do you
think people can change?
JIMMY.   Change what?
ANNIE.   Just *change.* You know, themselves. Who they are.
JIMMY.   Why?
ANNIE.   I was just thinking.
JIMMY.   I got a wife who *thinks.* Why are you thinking so
much?
ANNIE.   I couldn't sleep. *(Beat.)* If I never got pregnant,
Jimmy, do you think we'd still be together? I mean, or do you
think we would've broken up by now?
JIMMY.   Who knows?
ANNIE.   I'm just wondering.
JIMMY.   That's, like, an unanswerable question, Annie.
ANNIE.   Do you still love me?
JIMMY.   What? What's with all the *questions?*
ANNIE.   Do you still love me?
JIMMY.   What do you think?
ANNIE.   I want to *know.* Never mind what I think.
JIMMY.   If you can't tell, then it doesn't really matter, does
it?
ANNIE.   Sometimes it's nice to hear it.
JIMMY.   It's just a word, Annie. I mean, you got people on
TV swearing that they love turkey stuffing, or mouthwash.

People say they love songs on the radio. It's just a word, and anybody can use it. It's nothing special.

ANNIE.   But you used to tell me all the time. You must have told me over a hundred times on prom night alone. "I love you, I love you, I love you." Like the Beatles or something.

JIMMY.   You have to say "love" at the prom. It's like a state law or something.

ANNIE.   I'm serious, Jimmy.

JIMMY.   Annie, I wanted you to be there when I woke up from a bad dream. If that's not love, I don't know what to tell you.

ANNIE.   Just tell me you love me.

JIMMY.   Can I *show* you?

ANNIE.   How?

JIMMY.   Like this. *(Jimmy kisses Annie. Annie breaks from the kiss and hands Jimmy a glass of juice she's been drinking.)*

ANNIE.   Here.

JIMMY.   What's this for?

ANNIE.   Sleepy breath. *(Jimmy drinks some juice, gargles with it, swallows it. He kisses Annie again.)*

JIMMY.   How's that?

ANNIE.   Better. *(They kiss. This kiss is longer than the others. When it ends, Jimmy curls up in Annie's arms once again, resting his head on her.)*

JIMMY.   *(Quietly.)* Annie. *(Recites like a nursery rhyme.)* Annie, Annie, Little Orphan Annie ...

ANNIE.   Jimmy, Jimmy, Little Orphan ... Jimmy ...

Scene Seven

The den. Jimmy is pacing. Grandmother is in her wheelchair, flipping through TV Guide. *Annie walks in.*

ANNIE.   Jimmy, have you seen Wendy's Barbie doll in here?

JIMMY.   No.

ANNIE.   Have you seen it *anywhere?*

JIMMY.   No.
ANNIE.   *(Beat.)* Is something wrong?
JIMMY.   No. *(Beat.)* I'm going outside. *(Jimmy walks out.)*
ANNIE.   Good talking to you. *(Beat.)* Grandma, is something the matter with Jimmy?
GRANDMOTHER.   It's the day.
ANNIE.   What day? Today?
GRANDMOTHER.   His parents died today.
ANNIE.   What? Oh, what, it's the anniversary?
GRANDMOTHER.   Today is, yes.
ANNIE.   I'm sorry. I didn't know that. I'm sorry.
GRANDMOTHER.   Did you kill them?
ANNIE.   What?
GRANDMOTHER.   Did you kill them?
ANNIE.   No.
GRANDMOTHER.   So don't be sorry.
ANNIE.   Sorry.
GRANDMOTHER.   If Jimmy's *father* were still here — Jimmy's father was an *angel* ...
ANNIE.   Jimmy never talks about his father — he never talks about his parents with me.
GRANDMOTHER.   You have to earn the right to know.
ANNIE.   I'm his *wife.*
GRANDMOTHER.   You're his *wife*, sure, but you weren't there. You didn't have to go through it with him. Try sleeping when a little boy screams through the night, hitting and kicking the walls. Try telling him he's an *orphan.*
ANNIE.   But he had *you* —
GRANDMOTHER.   He's an *orphan.* His parents are *dead.* *(Grandmother looks away from Annie and starts reading* TV Guide. *Pause. Annie walks over to the window.)*
ANNIE.   *(Beat.)* I'm gonna let some sunlight in here.
GRANDMOTHER.   It ruins the TV picture. It makes a glare.
ANNIE.   But it's so bleak in here, Grandma, sometimes it's so bleak. I have to take Wendy outside to show her some light.
GRANDMOTHER.   I don't want the window shades open. I can see sunlight on television.

Scene Eight

*The den. Jimmy is sitting on the floor. Scattered around are
an old manual typewriter, some cassette tapes, a tape recorder
and some beer cans — a few empty, a few unopened. Jimmy
presses a button on the tape recorder.*

JIMMY.   A Detective Story. By James Oswald Bonaparte. Tape
number one. Christmas Eve 1984. Annie and Wendy are at
Annie's parent's place. Grandma's out of the way. This is *my*
time. I'm gonna talk the story into this tape recorder. I have
plenty of tapes here, enough to get me through the night, I
think, and some beer which I have been drinking already so
I am a bit drunk, a little, but not really, and, in any case, it
won't get in the way of the story, which is gonna be fabulous.
(Pause.) Uhh, okay. The title of this story — this *detective* story,
it's title is going to be — umm, for now, for a *working* title,
I will call it "The Blonde With A Big Chest." Yeah. But that's
just for now. I'll change it eventually. Okay. It starts off with
this guy, umm, he looks sort of like me, only he has a *mous-
tache,* and he's wearing *suspenders.* And a *hat.* Which he wears,
without even trying to do it like this, but he has it always kind
of raked over one eye. His *left* eye. Yeah, his *left* eye. And he's
sitting in his dark detective's office in the Big City, and he's
reading his name written backwards on the window plate, and
he's drinking. Just like always, he's drinking a beer. No, he's
drinking — *scotch.* Mixed with *gin.* A *hard* drink. Tastes like
shit, but makes him feel like a *man.* And he *is* a man. He's
just a little *down,* a little *beaten.* Like *anybody.* Lots of bottles
on his desk, and his feet are right in the center of them.
Bottle of vodka, bottle of rum, bottle of tequila, and cham-
pagne, bottle of — bottle of *liqueur,* real *fancy,* even a bottle
of *mineral* water. All of them *empty.* Even the mineral water. *Especially* the fucking *mineral* water. Oh, and there's also a bottle
of virgin's blood, but he keeps it in one of his file cabinets.
There are *lots* of file cabinets in the office, all around. And
he's really *sad.* Close to *tears,* I mean, but he will definitely *not*

cry. Never. And he's thinking in his head of a better *time*. And especially of this blonde with a big chest. Hence the title, right? And, uhh, like, he's thinking she'll come in his door, you know, even though his office looks closed, she'll come in and say, "Mr. Detective, I need *help*. I just need *help*. *Help* me." Except she'll sound different. More — *better*. Like, umm — *(Annie walks in, wearing a blonde wig and — underneath her dress — a padded bra.)*
ANNIE.   Mr. Detective, I need *help*. I just need *help*. *Help* me.
JIMMY.   And he looks up to see her, and she's fucking *great* looking, *real* expensive and cheap at the same time, and she *wants* him. I mean, it's like written all over her — *chest*. *(Annie undoes the top of her dress. "I Want You" is written on her bra.)* He lifts the rake of his hat up so he can use both eyes to perceive *depth*. She is something *else*. Something else from *anything* else. He tries to keep cool. He says, "I am a detective. Can I help you with any detective type services?" She says —
ANNIE.   Yes. Yes, I think so. You see, I've *lost* something.
JIMMY.   "You've *lost* something," he says. "I see. What is it that you have lost, if I may ask?" She tells him —
ANNIE.   Of course you may ask. I've lost —
JIMMY.   Shit, *what* has she lost? It has to *be* something. I'll figure it out later, the mechanical stuff. He says he'll help her, they talk about payment, all her money is, uhh, is *tied up* in, uhh, *investments*, but —
ANNIE.   I really need help. Perhaps there is some *way* —
JIMMY.   There *is* some way. Of *course* there is going to be some way. This is going to be the best goddamn detective story *ever*. This is *great!* It's clicking into place like *marbles* or something, like marbles falling into *grooves*. He talks some more, real suave, gets up, goes to her. *(Jimmy gets up and goes to Annie.)* Kisses her. *(Jimmy kisses Annie.)* Runs his fingers through her luscious blonde hair like a professional *stylist*. *(Jimmy runs his fingers through Annie's blonde wig. It comes off into his hand.)* He holds her hair in his hands and looks at it for a good, long moment. *(Jimmy looks at the blonde wig for a long moment.)* Annie! What the *fuck* are you doing in my story? In my *thoughts*. *My* thoughts. You look like a fucking *whore*.

ANNIE.   Face it, Jimmy. You want to be a dreamer in the *movies* or something, like Robert *DeNiro*, Jimmy. You're not Robert DeNiro, Jimmy. You're not even *Italian*. And you're not in the movies. You don't have the right genealogy. You're just a *dreamer*. *(Jimmy throws the blonde wig on the floor. Annie picks it up and walks out.)*
GRANDMOTHER.   *(Off.)* Jimmy! What are you doing?
JIMMY.   *Huh? Nothing,* Grandma.
GRANDMOTHER.   *(Off.)* Who the hell are you *talking* to?
JIMMY.   My fucking *self.* Go back to sleep.
GRANDMOTHER.   *(Off.)* Are you going to be quiet now?
JIMMY.   *What?*
GRANDMOTHER.   *(Off.)* Are you going to *shut up?*
JIMMY.   *You* shut up. Go to sleep.
GRANDMOTHER.   *(Off.)* I *was* asleep.
JIMMY.   Find your way *back. Shit. (Pause.)* Shit, shit, *shit. (Pause.)* I lost my fucking *place.*

Scene Nine

The den. Grandmother is in her wheelchair, knitting. Annie is sitting in a chair, sipping a drink. Jimmy walks in, carrying a small paper bag.

JIMMY.   It's *freezing* out there. There's ice on *everything.*
GRANDMOTHER.   Coldest day this winter. Said on the News.
JIMMY.   You don't have to watch the News to find *that* out. Just go *outside.*
GRANDMOTHER.   Did you pick up my prescription?
JIMMY.   Yeah. Here. *(Jimmy takes a bottle of pills from the bag and hands it to Grandmother.)*
GRANDMOTHER.   We've got more termites.
JIMMY.   Great. Just what I need. They're like *toying* with me now, showing up on the surface, not giving a shit who sees, dancing around. They're in the *skeleton* of this fucking house.

'Course, I don't even know if this *qualifies* as a house anymore. *(Grandmother wheels herself out.)*

ANNIE.   What else did you get?

JIMMY.   I got some vitamin C's, some Flintstones Chewables, and some aspirins, on account of you giving me a frigging fucking *headache* — What Else Is New?

ANNIE.   Jimmy, I want a divorce.

JIMMY.   *What?* Just 'cause I said you gave me a *headache?*

ANNIE.   No, that's not why, although it does have something to do with it, but not *specifically*, you know?

JIMMY.   What the fuck are you talking about?

ANNIE.   I'm talking about *that*. About you talking to me like I'm *dirt*. About you and me yelling at each other *always*. *Always*, Jimmy. It's a constant thing, and I hate it. It's not life. It's not marriage. It's a *fight*.

JIMMY.   People fight when they're married. It's part of being alive. It's *normal*.

ANNIE.   Maybe when it's balanced by some *good* stuff, but we never have good stuff, Jimmy, just fights. We never should have gotten married.

JIMMY.   I said that *years* ago. Why didn't you *listen?*

ANNIE.   I don't know. We *had* to get married. It was all I could do. I was really terrified, you know.

JIMMY.   So was I, okay? Don't make me seem like the bad guy.

ANNIE.   I'm not trying to do that, Jimmy. Don't put words into my mouth.

JIMMY.   How can you get divorced if you're *Catholic?*

ANNIE.   Don't *start*, Jimmy.

JIMMY.   *You* don't start. You never *should* have started. I would have been better off. But *no*. You made me marry you.

ANNIE.   I didn't *make* you do anything, Jimmy —

JIMMY.   You fucking *did*. And because of that, I wake up every morning from *horrible* dreams and you know what I see? I see this *world*. Of *possibilities*. And next to it, a huge brick wall. And then, over here, there's me. That's how I see it. That's life to me.

ANNIE.   I'm sorry you're feeling *bad*, but I'm feeling bad,

too.
JIMMY.   What the hell is *that?* You sound like a sympathy card I bought in the drug store. Don't feel *sorry* for me. I don't need that. I just need a quiet room where I can be alone with my thoughts, away from *you.*
ANNIE.   I'm *giving* you that, Jimmy, that's what I'm talking about.
JIMMY.   What are you gonna do?
ANNIE.   Move back in with my folks for a while. I don't know exactly what I'll do, but I'll do *something.* I'm not stupid, you know.
JIMMY.   No, *I'm* the one who's stupid.
ANNIE.   Jimmy —
JIMMY.   What about *Wendy?*
ANNIE.   *(Pause.)* What about her?
JIMMY.   Are you going to take her away from me?
ANNIE.   I want to raise her, yes.
JIMMY.   You're going to take my little girl away from me, too, huh?
ANNIE.   Jimmy, I'm not going to take her to *Alaska*, I'm going to take her to my parents' house. We'll be a few blocks away. You can see her whenever you want. I'm not trying to split the two of *you* up. Just the two of *us.*
JIMMY.   *Why?*
ANNIE.   Because this isn't going to be what the rest of my life is like. It can't be. I can't keep *doing* this. *(Long pause.)* What are you thinking about, Jimmy?
JIMMY.   Those plates we made in kindergarten.
ANNIE.   What?
JIMMY.   You remember those plates.
ANNIE.   *What* plates?
JIMMY.   Remember when we were in — what was her name?
ANNIE.   Miss Stouffel?
JIMMY.   Remember when we were in Miss Stouffel's class together?
ANNIE.   Yes.
JIMMY.   And one day, we all made these drawings on a special piece of paper, all the kids, and Miss Stouffel collected

them and a while later this pile of plates arrived, and you could eat off a plate with your drawing on it.
ANNIE.   I do remember that.
JIMMY.   It was cool. Anything's cool when you're *five*, you know? I did mine in purple and black ink. Just me as a little stick figure guy with enormous shoes on and no hands, and this house in the background, with a door and three windows and a chimney, and some grass at the bottom, this sort of *purple* grass, and my name written up in the sky. *James.* Real formal like. In real shitty handwriting. My folks were still around. And it was just this *plate* that was *mine.* (*Pause.*) I got in a fight and threw it and it broke apart. *Sucks.* It'd be kind of cool to eat off it again. Right now.
ANNIE.   I don't know *what* I did with my plate.
JIMMY.   You probably *devoured* it whole.
ANNIE.   What's that supposed to mean?
JIMMY.   Forget it, nothing, just forget it. Forget everything. *So.* When are you getting the hell *out?*
ANNIE.   Jimmy, don't *be* like that.
JIMMY.   I'll be like whatever I want to be like. I'm a single man now, right? (*Jimmy shuts his eyes tight for a moment.*)
ANNIE.   What's the matter?
JIMMY.   My head is *pounding* from this shit. (*Jimmy reaches into the bag.*)
ANNIE.   Take some aspirins.
JIMMY.   Aww, thanks for the advice. What does it *look* like I'm doing? (*Jimmy takes an aspirin bottle from the bag and unscrews the cap. He reads the safety seal.*) "Sealed For Your Protection." Sealed for my protection. *Huh.* Hey, honey, if there'd been one of these here things over your cunt when I first met you, we never would've gotten ourselves into all this messy shit. (*Annie throws her drink in Jimmy's face.*) Okay, I guess that's right, I guess I deserve a wet face, okay. (*Jimmy breaks the safety seal, takes out two aspirins and swallows them.*)
ANNIE.   I'm leaving.
JIMMY.   *Don't ...* (*Beat. Annie walks over to Jimmy and touches his cheek with her hand. Beat. She starts to put her arms around him.*) Don't.

ANNIE. I just want to —
JIMMY. Don't do that.
ANNIE. Why not?
JIMMY. Just don't.
ANNIE. Why *not?*
JIMMY. Just don't.
ANNIE. *Why?*
JIMMY. Just ...

Scene Ten

A Mexican divorce court. Jimmy and Annie are standing before a Divorce Guy.

DIVORCE GUY. Verdaderamente me hace triste que en un mundo tan destrozado, y en un mundo donde hace falta communión, dos jovenes tan simpáticos como ustedes no han logrado arreglar sus problemas. *Ahh, well.* Asi pasan las cosas. Y que hago si soy un romantico perdido? Un divorcio es tan dependable como la muerte hoy en dia. Y no hay razón que nadie pueda consegir un divorcio rapido y sin dolor. No hay razón. Entonces, yo accepto esa pocisión. La pocisión de ser el que os separa. El que divorcia hombre de mujer, esposo de esposa. *Ahh, well.* Con el poder vestido en mi, pronuncio qué, con pagamiento al salir que no serais esposo y esposa. Este matrimonio ha desolvado. Su divorcio será honorado.
JIMMY. *(Pause.)* Umm, so, are we divorced or *what?*

Scene Eleven

The supermarket. Jimmy and Arturo are putting price stickers on cans.

JIMMY. Do you ever have *dreams?*
ARTURO. Sure.

JIMMY.   What sort of dreams do you have?
ARTURO.   I just dream of stuff. People I know. People I
know talking to other people I know, but they don't know
each other in real life, so it's a little weird. Stuff like that.
JIMMY.   You ever have daydreams?
ARTURO.   Dreaming during the day?
JIMMY.   Yeah. Daydreams.
ARTURO.   No.
JIMMY.   Never?
ARTURO.   Dreaming during the *day?*
JIMMY.   Yeah, during the day.
ARTURO.   No.
JIMMY.   I just, I don't know, sometimes I'm doing something
and I just start, you know, *drifting,* and suddenly I'm some-
where entirely *else,* you know, thinking of something I want to
be or *do,* something *more,* and I don't know, I don't know if
it's good or bad or *what?* I mean, if I *should* be doing it, why
not *do* it? Why am I *thinking* about it?
ARTURO.   Oh, you mean *thoughts.* I have *thoughts* during the
day, yeah.
JIMMY.   Like what sort of thoughts?
ARTURO.   I don't know. About stuff later in the day, plans
and stuff.
JIMMY.   Oh. *(Pause.)* How's your girlfriend doing?
ARTURO.   She's okay.
JIMMY.   Good. *(Pause.)* What's her name?
ARTURO.   Sally.
JIMMY.   *Sally. (Pause.)* That's good. *(Pause.)* I dream a lot. I
dream in the supermarket all the time. I dream of *buying* the
fucking supermarket. Just buying it and *owning* it and, I don't
know, taking a piss on the potato chip section or something,
you know, and not having to *give* a shit. *(Pause.) Dreaming.
(Pause.)* I dream *constantly,* dream of doing all kinds of shit,
you know. *Amazing* stuff. I dream too *much,* maybe. *No.* But,
you know, I saw a movie once, and at one point, a guy is
climbing a mountain or something, but not with rope and all
of that stuff, just in normal clothes, and there's this shot of
him *surrounded* by white fucking snow everywhere, nothing for

goddamn *miles* around, just this *guy. Climbing,* trying to *get* somewhere. And, you know, sometimes I think *I'm* that guy, moving around, nothing different from anything, trying to *get* somewhere. And then I fucking kick my head, because I'm not *even* that guy in the movie, climbing in the middle of white snow everywhere, I'm not *even* him, because I'm *thinking* of him. See? It drives me up a wall. A fucking *wall.*
ARTURO.   Or a mountain.
JIMMY.   Huh?
ARTURO.   It drives you up a wall or a *mountain.*
JIMMY.   Yeah. Yeah, or up a mountain, too. I just, sometimes it fucking gets *inside* me, it *really* gets to me.
ARTURO.   *(Pause.)* Me and Sally broke up, actually.
JIMMY.   Huh? You *what?*
ARTURO.   My girlfriend, Sally. And me. We broke up last week.
JIMMY.   Oh. *(Pause.)* That sucks. I'm sorry.
ARTURO.   That's okay. You know. *(Pause.)* How's your daughter?
JIMMY.   Wendy?
ARTURO.   Yeah.
JIMMY.   She's doing good. You know, when I get the chance, I see her. She's a beautiful kid. Seven years old now, you know. She's *good.*
ARTURO.   You and your wife still broken up?
JIMMY.   We didn't break up, Arturo, we got *divorced.*
ARTURO.   Well, same thing.
JIMMY.   Yeah, I guess. Yeah, we're still divorced.
ARTURO.   Sorry.
JIMMY.   It's *okay,* Arturo. It's been a while since. It's *okay.*
ARTURO.   Yeah. *(Pause.)* Women.
JIMMY.   *Women. (Pause.)* You ever gonna come see me at the Laugh Riot?
ARTURO.   Oh, yeah. When is that again? I always forget.
JIMMY.   Every other week. On Tuesday. Once every two weeks.
ARTURO.   How is that?
JIMMY.   I keep telling you to come *see* it. You'll *see* how it is.

ARTURO.   Yeah, I'll try. You do tell me. You always tell me.
I just forget. I forget stuff all the time.
JIMMY.   You should try to remember stuff, Arturo. It's *important.*
ARTURO.   Yeah, I will. I'll try to remember stuff. *(Pause.)*
Tuesday?

Scene Twelve

*The Laugh Riot's stage. Jimmy walks on and picks up the
microphone.*

JIMMY.   Pleasure to be here at the Laugh Riot's bi-weekly
amateur night. I'm Jimmy Bonaparte, and ice cream runs
through my veins. My sixth grade teacher told me that and
I've never been able to forget it, especially since every time I
get a paper cut, something pink that tastes like strawberry
comes out instead of blood. Yeah, I had a weird sixth grade
teacher. I had a weird sixth *grade.* Come to think of it, I had
a weird *childhood.* My parents were *weird.* They died when I
was little, and, you know, sometimes I thank *God* for that, because if they were alive, they'd have influenced me, and I'd
be *weird,* and that would *suck.* I want to be normal. But I
didn't come from normal parents. *From Leave It To Beaver* parents. "June, all of Beaver's *teeth* have fallen out!" "*Leave* it to
Beaver, Ward, they're just *teeth,* he'll deal with it by putting
them under his *pillow* and waiting for them to be taken by
the Tooth Fairy, who might just hop into the sack with Little
Ol' Beav' while he's collecting the teeth and give him a *blow*
job, 'cause after all, a fairy's a fairy, even if it's the Tooth
Fairy, and anyway, I think it's about time little old Beaver
learned about homosexuality and deviance, and, heck, if we
bring Good Ol' Wally into the bed, we can add group sex and
incest as *well.*" Real stereotypical *good* parents. Real *normal*
parents. Of course, there's always the problem of the old
Switcherooney. Which is what happens when normal people —

like myself — think everything's going pretty well and they're somewhere kind of good, kind of close to where they want to be and they're feeling pretty good about themselves and all of a sudden — *Switcherooney* — and everybody flipped over backwards, changed positions, and they're all waving at you from all the way across the room, all the way over there, laughing at you, saying, "Boy, did we fuck *you* up. You worked so hard to get to where you are — *fooled* ya. The Magic Spot ain't over there, it's over *here* now, fooled you *bad,* sucker, *fuck* you, *moron.* Ha, *ha!*" The Good Ol' Switcherooney — just like Good Ol' Beaver Cleaver. "Thought you were a little boy, Beav'? Well, tough shit, bullcrap, we fooled you, you're growing breasts and you're a little *girl,* take off the baseball cap, grow long hair, have kids, change your life, you little shit, we *got* your white ass." Oh, *well. Normal* stuff. Anyhow, this is my seventh year coming to amateur night. Thank you. Nothing like being an amateur for seven years. Except, of course, being an amateur for *seventy* years. Let's hope *that's* not me. Oh, fucking *God.* Well, what the fuck, that's okay. I've discovered the Perfect Rim Shot in my seven years here at the Laugh Riot. It goes like this — but you have to follow closely, 'cause things turn into *other* things — there's the typical rim shot drum sound to start it: bah-dum-bum-*chhhhoooom* and the drum turned into an airplane taking off and suddenly I'm in the bathroom in the back of the plane with a *hot* fucking stewardess, *naked,* serving me Bloody Mary's from her *tray* — but *wait* — the airplane is just an image on the TV screen of an old woman on a couch who leans forward and — *click.* (*Pause.*) *Gone.* (*Pause.*) Oh, *well.* I'm Jimmy Bonaparte. Thanks a lot. (*Jimmy drops the microphone and walks off.*)

Scene Thirteen

The den. Jimmy and Tralice walk in.

JIMMY.   Sit down. You want a beer or something?

TRALICE.   A beer sounds good.

JIMMY.   And tastes even *better.* Wait right here. *(Jimmy walks out. Tralice sits. Jimmy walks in after a moment with two cans of beer. He opens one and hands it to Tralice. He opens the other one.)* A toast. To — to *you.*

TRALICE.   Thanks. *(They knock their beer cans together. They both take a sip of beer. Jimmy sits next to Tralice.)*

JIMMY.   So, *Tralice.* Here we are.

TRALICE.   Your act tonight was *really* funny.

JIMMY.   I made you laugh?

TRALICE.   Yeah. Yeah, you did. It was *strange.*

JIMMY.   What was your favorite part of it?

TRALICE.   I really liked the *Leave It To Beaver* jokes. They were funny. I — that's a funny thing to make fun of. I could never get up there and take the microphone and try to make people laugh.

JIMMY.   It's tough to do. Of course, the audience at the Laugh Riot on a Tuesday — well, I don't have to tell you. They fucking *suck.*

TRALICE.   Yeah. They don't tip too well. None of the customers ever tip too well, but Tuesday's *real* low.

JIMMY.   Amateur night, I guess. None of the fucking *pros.*

TRALICE.   Yeah.

JIMMY.   I've *seen* the pros, you know, I've *gone* on a Saturday night and *watched,* you know, to try to *learn,* to try to *grow,* but they're all doing shit. In fact, it's worse than on Tuesday, because they don't even wonder if they're good or not. They *know* they're good, but they're *not* good, so they have no fucking defenses and just plow ahead with bad *shit.* If that's comedy on Saturday night at the Laugh Riot in the heart of New Fucking Jersey, I must be God or something.

TRALICE.   Yeah, I know what you mean.

JIMMY.   Stop me if I start going off, it's just a subject that gets me fired up. *Passionate*, you know?

TRALICE.   Yeah. And it *should.* I understand. It means a lot to you.

JIMMY.   Yeah, it does, you're right. *(Pause.)* How *old* are you, Tralice?

TRALICE.   Me? Eighteen. Why?

JIMMY.   No, no reason.

TRALICE.   Oh. *(Pause.)* How old are *you?*

JIMMY.   *Me?* You kidding?

TRALICE.   No. How old? Come *on.*

JIMMY.   I'm twenty-seven.

TRALICE.   Twenty-seven. *Hmm.*

JIMMY.   *(Pause.)* Why? That seem *old?*

TRALICE.   *No. (Pause.)* Does eighteen seem young?

JIMMY.   No, no. Eighteen seems just *right. (Jimmy kisses Tralice.)* You still in high school?

TRALICE.   No. I got out last year. *(Jimmy kisses Tralice.)* Put down your beer, Jimmy. *(Jimmy puts down his beer can and Tralice puts down hers. Tralice kisses Jimmy, putting her hands in his hair. After a moment, he puts his arms around her. After a few moments, they break from the kiss.)*

JIMMY.   They taught you well at high school. *(They start to kiss again. Grandmother wheels herself in, looks at Jimmy and Tralice kissing for a moment, then wheels herself across and out — into the kitchen. A few moments later, Jimmy and Tralice break from the kiss.)* You're a hell of a kisser. Soft lips.

TRALICE.   So do you.

JIMMY.   I do? Soft?

TRALICE.   Yeah. Really soft. Nice.

JIMMY.   Hey. How do you like that? Nobody ever told me I had soft lips before.

TRALICE.   There's a first time for everything, even when you're twenty-seven.

JIMMY.   I think I read that on a bathroom wall once. I was throwing up.

TRALICE.   You're *sick.*

JIMMY.   Why you say that? Just 'cause I got a *thermometer* sticking out my ass?

TRALICE. *(Laughing.)* That's not funny.

JIMMY. So don't laugh. If you laugh, I say it's funny. If not, *not. Simple. (Pause.)* Hey, how'd you get the name Tralice? What kind of a name is that?

TRALICE. When my mother was pregnant with me, a man named Tommy Reilly helped her change a flat tire. She said she'd name me Thomas if I were a boy and T.R. Alice if I were a girl, since she was set on Alice for a girl. So I was a girl, and it was Alice with a. T.R. tacked on the front to honor Tommy Reilly. Kind of stupid.

JIMMY. Nah. It's a nice name. *Distinctive.* I like that. Naming kids is a funny thing. *(Pause.)* You're lucky *I* didn't help your mother with the flat. Your name would have been *Jbalice.* J for Jimmy, B for Bonaparte, Alice for Alice. Jbalice. Can barely fucking *pronounce* it.

TRALICE. Yeah, well, you would have been, like, *nine* when I was born. Were you changing tires at nine?

JIMMY. Baby, I was *eating* tires at nine. I was doing shit at nine you could never even *dream* of. Nine was a good year. *(Pause.)* Now, *ten,* on the other hand, ten —

TRALICE. Cut it out.

JIMMY. Hey, this is good comedy here.

TRALICE. Kiss me.

JIMMY. Then again, a kiss is always better than a joke. *(Jimmy kisses Tralice.)* I tell you I'm going onto television soon?

TRALICE. What? No, you didn't say anything about that.

JIMMY. Yeah. I am.

TRALICE. Well, *tell* me.

JIMMY. I'm going to get onto the public access channel, you know, on cable.

TRALICE. We don't get cable.

JIMMY. No cable? *Shit. Everybody* has cable.

TRALICE. I guess we're not everybody.

JIMMY. You don't want to be, neither. Well, you can come over here and watch it. It's gonna be great. I'm gonna have a phone where people can call in and stuff and I'll talk to them sind hang up on them and all of that, and I'll do my routines and all kinds of great shit.

TRALICE.   That sounds great. How'd you work that out?
JIMMY.   I just pay some money for each show and they have some guys at the local station who'll do the video and the technical stuff for me. The cable people are happy as hell to give you time if you pay them a little for it. They made TV so great, with so many fucking *channels*, then some moron turned around and realized, *shit*, we have to make stuff to put on to *fill* all these great channels now. You know, like channel ninety-one and shit like that. *(Pause.)* Just you *wait*.
TRALICE.   I will.
JIMMY.   *(Pause.)* You want a banana?
TRALICE.   Are you having one?
JIMMY.   Yeah, I think I'm in the mood for one.
TRALICE.   Yeah, sure, I'll have one.
JIMMY.   Plus, I got this great trick to teach you with it, I think you'll learn it really quick, it's *easy*. And *fun*. Just like *me*.
TRALICE.   Oh, you're *dirty*, Jimmy.
JIMMY.   Dirty? Maybe I need to take a *shower*. Want to come?
TRALICE.   Maybe later.
JIMMY.   You serious?
TRALICE.   Sure. You?
JIMMY.   Uhh, *sure. Definitely* sure. Very definitely sure, yes. I'll be back.
TRALICE.   I'll be here. *(Jimmy kisses Tralice, then walks out — into the kitchen.)*
JIMMY.   *(Off.)* Get your rotted hands off my fucking *beer*. *(Tralice looks at the beer can in her hand.)*

Scene Fourteen

The den. Grandmother is in her wheelchair, watching Jimmy's show on cable television.

JIMMY.   *(On television.)* You're so full of it, pal, you're going to *burst*. Like a *balloon*. You're a *balloon*. And I've had enough of you. You're *gone*. Yes? Hello?
CALLER.   *(On television.)* Jimmy?

JIMMY.   (On television.) Yeah. Who are you?
CALLER.   (On television.) What do you care? You *suck*.
JIMMY.   (On television.) Oh, *wow*. That's *inventive*.
CALLER.   (On television.) You're not the American Dream. You're a *turd*.
JIMMY.   (On television.) Oh, wow, you feel *big*, huh? You get to almost *swear* on cable television. You feel *big*?
CALLER.   (On television.) *Turd*.
JIMMY.   (On television.) You're a turd's turd, how do you like that?
CALLER.   (On television.) I like that better than I like you or your dumb, pointless show.
JIMMY.   (On television.) Suck my Grandma's tit, okay?
CALLER.   (On television.) Your Grandma must have flies nesting in her butt. I bet she has an *ant* colony up her butt. I bet *you* could fit up your Grandma's butt.
JIMMY.   (On television.) Hey, shut up about my Grandma's butt. Only *I* can say shit like that about my Grandma, okay. *Got* it?
CALLER.   (On television.) Your Grandma goes to the movies and tries to give head to the actors on the screen. The *women*, too. Your Grandma eats dog shit with catsup. Your Grandma is *your* Grandma. I think you know what I mean. *(Grandmother shakes her head, wheels herself forward and clicks the television set off.)*

Scene Fifteen

The supermarket. Jimmy and Arturo are putting price stickers on cans.

JIMMY.   God, I *hate* putting these fucking stickers on all this shit. It's so *tedious*, you know? All the fucking *time*.
ARTURO.   It's what we *do*.
JIMMY.   It's not *all* I do, it's not *what* I do, it's a *thing* I do, and I still fucking *hate* it. I'd like to put a price sticker on the fucking *boss*, you know, just put a price sticker on him, a real

low one, buy him for pocket change, put him in a food processor and make a *salad.* Boss Salad. That'd probably taste great.

ARTURO.   Probably not, if you really *did* it.

JIMMY.   Yeah, of course not, if I did it *really.* I'm just saying.

ARTURO.   Oh.

JIMMY.   *(Pause.)* Fucking *tired* as all hell.

ARTURO.   Did you sleep last night?

JIMMY.   Not enough. Did the show again — my twentieth show, you know that?

ARTURO.   Yeah?

JIMMY.   Yeah. Not so bad for an amateur, right? I bet they ask me to do a regular spot at the Laugh Riot soon. With the show and all, I mean, it seems logical. We'll see. But *fuck,* you know, it wears you out, this stuff. *Doing* stuff.

ARTURO.   Yeah. Everything wears you out if you do it long enough.

JIMMY.   That's the fucking truth. I shouldn't have drunk last night at all, you know, I know better, but I did anyhow. You know that waitress I was seeing?

ARTURO.   With the funny name.

JIMMY.   Tralice.

ARTURO.   Tralice. Yes.

JIMMY.   Yeah. That's over with.

ARTURO.   What happened?

JIMMY.   Well, you know, *nothing,* really. She was saving up money for school for a year, you know, and waitressing, and she did her year, and her folks are putting up some of the money, too, so she left for school. So she's gone. Last night was her last night around, so she was over, and we drank a lot.

ARTURO.   She's going to school today?

JIMMY.   Yeah. Remember when September meant another school year was starting and all of that? Now, it's just September. Again.

ARTURO.   My birthday's this month.

JIMMY.   Yeah? When?

ARTURO.   September fifth.

JIMMY.   That past already. Why didn't you tell me it was your birthday?

ARTURO.   I don't know.

JIMMY.   How old you turn?

ARTURO.   Twenty-eight.

JIMMY.   Yeah. Same as me. *(Pause.)* Happy Birthday.

ARTURO.   Thanks.

JIMMY.   Yeah. Sure. *(Pause.)* I feel all tired and *drained*, you know? My eyes are watery a little, and my *lips* are dry, they feel all *crackly*, you know, and my teeth feel soft and taste like *shit*, you know? I *hate* being this tired.

ARTURO.   Yeah. You get a lot more sleep if you realize nobody has anything interesting to say.

JIMMY.   *(Pause.)* What the hell's that mean? That doesn't make any sense.

ARTURO.   I don't know. *I* get a lot of sleep.

JIMMY.   Yeah, and you get virtually *no* women.

ARTURO.   That's not true. I fucked a *virgin*, just the other night. What do you think of that?

JIMMY.   What do I think of *that*? I think it's *impossible*, that's what *I* think.

ARTURO.   You don't *believe* me, is that what you're saying?

JIMMY.   I'm saying you can't *fuck* a *virgin* — one term *denies* the other.

ARTURO.   You know what I mean. She was a virgin, *then* I fucked her.

JIMMY.   And so now she's not a virgin?

ARTURO.   Well, of *course* not. I just *said* I fucked her, didn't I?

JIMMY.   Yeah, how *old* was she, Arturo, huh? Was she *three*?

ARTURO.   Will you shut the hell up, Jimmy? She wasn't *three*. What's eating at you, huh?

JIMMY.   *Worms*. These big, gross, dark black worms with blonde wigs and razor fucking teeth, okay? I didn't get any *sleep*, I *told* you that. I'm *edgy*.

ARTURO.   Doesn't mean you have to be *mean*.

JIMMY.   Sorry I was *mean*, Arturo, sorry I hurt your *feelings*.

Congratulations on fucking a virgin. I hope she bled endlessly.
ARTURO.   (*Pause.*) How's your *daughter* doing?
JIMMY.   *Wendy?*
ARTURO.   Yeah.
JIMMY.   Wendy is doing *fine*, Arturo. She's fucking *beautiful* and I don't get to see her enough. She's nine years old. She's a *virgin.* Maybe you can *fuck* her, too. (*Pause.*) Have you even watched my show once yet, huh, or do you keep *forgetting?* It's on TV, you know, it's not like amateur night, you don't have to leave your fucking *couch.*
ARTURO.   Yeah, I saw it once. A few weeks ago. I didn't really like it.
JIMMY.   *Yeah?* Well, fuck *you*, Arturo. Alright? Just fuck *you*. (*Jimmy puts a price sticker on Arturo's forehead.*)

Scene Sixteen

The den. Jimmy is standing. Grandmother is in her wheelchair.

JIMMY.   I hate playing cards, Grandma. Play with .yourself. Play solitaire or something.
GRANDMOTHER.   What about Scrabble?
JIMMY.   No board games. Board games are for morons. The people who make the board games are a swarm of pathetic individuals, Grandma. They don't have any *vision.* No *dreams.* I mean, come on. The game of *Life?* Where the perfect girl looks like a faceless, formless little pink *peg?* What jerk came up with that one? Where you only win if you're a doctor with two-point-five kids and a car? I don't have to walk down to K Mart and pay ten bucks to know I've lost that game, thank you very much.
GRANDMOTHER.   Well, *what*, then? You tell me *what.*
JIMMY.   I don't know. Look, it ain't my job to entertain you, Grandma. I didn't bust the television set. Just because you can't survive without watching TV twenty-one hours a day

doesn't mean I have to be the entertaining babysitter while you wait for the repair guy. I got more important shit to take care of.

GRANDMOTHER.   Oh, yeah? Like what?

JIMMY.   I gotta practice my act before Wendy gets here. *(Pause.)* And I gotta drink another beer.

GRANDMOTHER.   Maybe if you stopped drinking beer they'd move you up from Amateur Night.

JIMMY.   Maybe if I stopped drinking beer, I'd sober up enough to realize that you're driving me nuts and I'd flush you down the toilet. There'd be a flood, and I could just float away on top of the water, away from all of this stuff.

GRANDMOTHER.   Go already. Nobody's stopping you, Big Man. Go.

JIMMY.   I'm going to get a beer. *(Jimmy walks out. A moment later, he walks back in drinking a beer, just as Annie walks in.)*

ANNIE.   Hello, Jimmy. Hello, Grandma.

GRANDMOTHER.   Hello.

JIMMY.   Annie. *(Pause.)* What's up? Where's Wendy?

ANNIE.   She's in bed, at home. At our house. She's got a cold.

JIMMY.   What are you doing, are you sending her out into the rain naked or something? The kid's nine years old, she's fragile. She could break or something.

ANNIE.   She's going to be fine. She's resting. And drinking lots of orange juice.

JIMMY.   Does she need any Nyquil or something? Anything I can get her?

ANNIE.   She's got it all under control. I get worried about her and she tells me I'm a hypochondriac. I couldn't *say* hypochondriac when I was nine.

JIMMY.   All you could say when you were nine was "Jimmy!" Waving at me across the playground.

ANNIE.   You were something back then.

JIMMY.   I'll swear, you were a pain in the ass.

ANNIE.   You paid attention to me, too. You gave me Valentine's cards all the time. I remember once in the first grade you gave me a Valentine's card in May. I never understood why. You ran away before I could ask.

JIMMY.   May, February, same fucking thing. A month's a month.

ANNIE.   I tried to call you, Jimmy, and let you know about Wendy, but something's messed up with your phone.

JIMMY.   It's on the list.

ANNIE.   What list?

JIMMY.   The list of broken stuff around here. The phone, the doorbell, the television, the drying machine, the toaster. Grandma over here.

GRANDMOTHER.   Be quiet, you louse.

JIMMY.   What? I don't think I've ever seen you work, so I just figure you must be broken. Is that a ridiculous assumption?

GRANDMOTHER.   *You're* a ridiculous assumption, Jimmy. *(Grandmother wheels herself out.)*

JIMMY.   You're Jack Fucking Benny, Grandma! You're The Three Fucking Stooges all rolled into one wheelchair!

ANNIE.   Jimmy, calm down.

JIMMY.   How am I supposed to calm down? I got a sick daughter, a house that's falling to pieces, and a grandmother with a slow wheelchair and a mighty fast fucking mouth. I can't calm down.

ANNIE.   Sure you could. You always could. You don't want to, that's all. You're afraid if you calm down somebody might get close to you.

JIMMY.   You left a whole shitload of tampons here, you know?

ANNIE.   What?

JIMMY.   There's a bunch of Super Tampax I found under the bathroom sink when I was looking for some Lysol. I made a pretty good guess that they're not Grandma's, considering she went through menopause when the Japanese bombed Pearl Harbor.

ANNIE.   You shouldn't joke about menopause, Jimmy. It's not funny.

JIMMY.   *Anything's* funny. You can joke about anything. *(Pause.)* Meno*pause*. What a stupid word. More like meno-*stop*, don't you think? It's a lot more final. Meno*pause* sounds like the lady expects to start getting her period again when she turns seventy-five.

ANNIE.   How did we get to menopause? I was talking about people getting close to you and you changed the subject. You see, Jimmy? You see how you do things like that?

JIMMY.   I let people get close to me. I got very close to this waitress. Very, very close, Annie. So don't give me any of this therapeutic crap.

ANNIE.   You got close to her knowing she'd be leaving for *school*, Jimmy. You'll only get close if there's a time limit on the relationship, is that it? What about with us?

JIMMY.   I got close to you, Annie. What are you going off about, saying I didn't get close to you? How did we manage to have a little girl without getting close? I'll get close to you right now. Come here.

ANNIE.   You're drunk.

JIMMY.   Who the fuck cares? I want to get close. I drank so I could calm down so I could get close to you. Come here, Annie.

ANNIE.   No.

JIMMY.   I want to kiss you. I want to kiss you like I used to. Like we did in high school. I want high school kisses.

ANNIE.   So do I.

JIMMY.   Come here.

ANNIE.   We can't have them, Jimmy. We can't *have* high school kisses. We're not there anymore. That's years ago. We can only have divorced kisses now, adult kisses.

JIMMY.   So? Okay. It's the same general principle. Two sets of lips coming together, a little moisture —

ANNIE.   A lot more responsibility. We could kiss. But, Jimmy, nobody yells at me anymore. Not at home. Not at work. Not at my night school. And I like it like that. *(Jimmy finishes his beer.)*

JIMMY.   Why don't you ever come see me anymore?

ANNIE.   What are you talking about, Jimmy? I'm right here.

JIMMY.   I mean *see* me. At the Laugh Riot.

ANNIE.   Jimmy, I told you. I have class on Tuesday.

JIMMY.   But my act has changed so much. You've never seen any of it. You could skip class on Tuesday.
ANNIE.   Jimmy, I can't.
JIMMY.   Annie, I'm telling you, it's a whole new act.
ANNIE.   For me too, Jimmy. I've got a whole new act for me, too. And I think it's working out pretty good.
JIMMY.   You're talking about your life, Annie. I'm really talking about my *act.* Don't get sentimental. I hate when you get all *soppy.*
ANNIE.   Jimmy —
JIMMY.   Grandma! Bring me a beer and get in here! I'm gonna practice!
ANNIE.   What?
JIMMY.   Sit down, Annie. If you can't bring yourself to the club, I'll bring the club to yourself. I've got a few new jokes, they're really great, you'll love them. Just sit on down. *(Annie sits. Grandmother wheels herself in and hands Jimmy a beer, which he opens and drinks. Jimmy dims the lights.)* Okay. *(Pause.)* Pleasure to be here at the Laugh Riot's bi-weekly amateur night. I'm Jimmy Bonaparte and ice cream runs through my veins. My sixth grade teacher told me that and I've never been able to forget it, especially since every time I get a paper cut something pink that tastes like strawberry comes out instead of blood. The other day, I spotted this really great looking change machine, and you know how it is when you see a really great looking change machine, I stuck my tongue inside the dollar bill changer and started to French kiss it a little. But all of a sudden — BOOM — my tongue seemed to disappear and I start to freak out, when all of a sudden four quarters come clinking out of the machine. This was when I realized that the whole thing was a sort of mirage, and I had my tongue intact. But I was really annoyed, because for that moment, I was pretty excited to get the four quarters so I could maybe buy a soda or something like that, but now all I had was my old tongue. Isn't that an odd word, "tongue"? I always used to be fascinated when I'd hear people order tongue in a restaurant or something. Kind of an old person's food. You never really see two young kids out on a date, the

guy's trying to impress the girl so he says to the waitress "We'll have two *tongue* sandwiches please, no lettuce." Doesn't happen. Only old people, like my fucking grandmother, order tongue. Let me tell you, I live with my wheelchair-bound grandmother, and if that ain't a joke, I don't know what is.
ANNIE. Jimmy, cut it out.
JIMMY. Oh, I see my ex-wife is heckling in the audience today. Huh, honey? Nice of you to make it. Good to see you. Reminds me of a touching story. My ex-wife is Catholic, and the Sunday after we got divorced, I was walking down the street past her church, and the doors were open, I guess so all the Jewish kids in the neighborhood could see what they were missing. So I walk up to the doors of the church, and there up front is my ex-wife Annie, on her knees, receiving Communion wafer, you know, where the priest is plopping this flavorless thing onto her tongue. *Tongue!* And I don't know what came over me, but I got this uncontrollable urge and I ran up the aisle and started to scream, "I was there first! My prick was in that mouth before your stupid Communion wafer! She blew me! That *Catholic* blew this Jew-Boy something *awful!* And she even *swallowed.*" (Pause.) So, you know, I guess I'm going to hell for that one.
ANNIE. Some things never change, Jimmy.
JIMMY. Oh, what, you mean like the fact that you never had a sense of humor and you never will?
ANNIE. You can think whatever you want to think, Jimmy. You can rant and rave and push me away, and push your grandmother away and push the world away. But I know you once gave me a Valentine's card in May.
JIMMY. Yeah, I know, Annie. And you know something? I wish I never did. It would have saved me a lot of pain if I just threw it down the sewer.
ANNIE. See, that's the difference right there, Jimmy. You wish you never gave me a Valentine's card. And I wish you never stopped. *(Annie hands Jimmy a small photograph.)* Here's Wendy's new school picture. She was going to give it to you herself. *(Pause.)* She's got your mouth. *(Pause.)* Bye, Grandma. *(Annie walks out.)*

JIMMY.   (Pause.) I swear, Grandma, some people wouldn't know a joke if it raped them in an alleyway. (Beat.) I gotta get out of this *house*.
GRANDMOTHER.   Jimmy, I don't feel good.
JIMMY.   I know Grandma. I *know* you don't feel good. *I* don't feel good. The *house* sure as hell don't feel good. Nothing feels good.
GRANDMOTHER.   I feel sick.
JIMMY.   What's the matter?
GRANDMOTHER.   Jimmy, I'm *sick.*
JIMMY.   What's the matter, Grandma? What's *wrong?*
GRANDMOTHER.   Jimmy, I'm *sick.*
JIMMY.   You *said* that, Grandma, I *know* that. I need to know what's *wrong.* You need to tell me what's the *matter.* I need to know what the *matter* is, Grandma. You need to *tell* me.
GRANDMOTHER.   I'm *sick.*
JIMMY.   Oh, Jesus. Oh, *fuck.*

Scene Seventeen

The Laugh Riot's stage. Jimmy walks on and picks up the microphone.

JIMMY.   Pleasure to be here at the Laugh Riot's bi-weekly amateur night. I'm Jimmy Bonaparte, and ice cream runs through my veins. My sixth grade teacher told me that and I've never been able to forget it, especially since every time I get a paper cut, something pink that tastes like strawberry comes out instead of blood. I've been opening with that for — a long time. Strawberry paper cut. Umm, *hmm.* Well. Uhh, I've got — I have a television show, I don't know, some of you may have seen it, it's on channel thirty-one. Thursday night at eleven-thirty. It's called *The American Dream,* uhh, and I just, I don't know, call me fucking crazy, I felt like plugging my own show up here, what *am* I? *Huh?* Uhh, so, uhh, *jokes,* on with the — the *funny* — the *jokes.* Uhh. Well, the other day, I stuck my tongue into the dollar bill space on a change machine, you know how it is when you see a really, uhh, good looking change machine, you start to French kiss it a little, and, uhh, all of a sudden my tongue was gone, or at least I thought it was, and I was fucking *terrified*, right, because I like my tongue. That's not funny. *(Pause.)* I can't make you people laugh, not even if I wanted to, which, well, really I kind of *don't*, but even if I *did*, you know? Nobody here ever *laughs*. I'm the Goddamn American Dream! But nobody ever laughs. Why do you people come? You never *laugh*. So I *pay* to have a TV show, and nobody gives a flying fuck about that either. *(Pause.)* A Flying Fuck. *What* an image. With parachutes or something. "Don't come till we're *about* to hit the ground, Honey." Ha, ha. That's not *funny! (Pause.)* I just put my grandmother into the fucking hospital — I just put my grandmother into the hospital to die, you know, 'cause that's what grandmothers *do* in hospitals, it's what they *do* — grandmothers *die* in hospitals, that's what they *do. She's* gonna die. And I can't make you fucking *laugh*. I mean, you know, I took my little girl to the hospital to see my Grandma, her Great-Grandma, and it's a really fucking scary place, the hospital, and she didn't flinch a second, she just made her way straight to the old lady and looked at her and there was — such *goodness. Fuck.* What *happens? Where* does the bad shit start *happening? (Pause.)* When I was young, I'd wait at my Grandma's bedside for her to wake up, holding a frying pan for scrambled eggs in one hand and a book by Dr. Seuss in the other hand. *Yertle The Turtle.* Great book. Every morning. Same book. Same frying pan. Same pajamas. Grandma never understood why I kept asking her to read the same book over and over — I think she got a little annoyed with me. She wasn't — she *isn't*, pardon me — she *isn't* a very *delicate* soul. "What is it about the book?" she'd want to know, but it wasn't anything about the book, it was her *reading* the book, and that feeling, knowing how she'd read it, that made me happy. *(Pause.)* I forget when Grandma stopped reading that book to me. I don't even know where the stupid book *is*. It's probably in the basement. Along with everything else. Right? *(Pause.) Right?*

(Pause.) RIGHT? *(Beat.)* No more jokes tonight. But if you want to laugh, go ahead.

Scene Eighteen

The den. Jimmy is standing, looking at Grandmother's wheelchair. Beat. He sits in the wheelchair. Long silence, broken by Wendy's voice offstage.

WENDY.   *(Off.)* Daddy! *(Wendy runs in.)* Daddy!
JIMMY.   Yeah, Wendy?
WENDY.   There's a cloud in the sky that looks just like you.
JIMMY.   Are you serious?
WENDY.   I swear. Come on. Come and see it.
JIMMY.   Show it to me.
WENDY.   Come on, Dad. Come on. *(Jimmy follows Wendy to the doorway. She runs out, but he stops in the doorway and turns to look at the empty wheelchair. Off.)* Daddy, come on!
JIMMY.   Coming. *(Jimmy walks out. The lights fade on the empty wheelchair.)*

END OF PLAY

PROPERTY LIST

Bifocals (Grandmother)
Glasses (Nurse)
Polaroid instant camera (Chapel Owner)
Picture taken from Polaroid (Chapel Owner)
Wedding bouquet (tacky Vegas-style) (Annie)
Bouquet of pretty flowers (simple) (Jimmy)
Newborn baby girl, swaddled (Jimmy)
Hospital tray
Hospital chart
4 pricing guns (2 from the 1970s; 2 modern) (Jimmy)
Inventory list
Pencil
2 market aprons
Knitting (Grandmother)
Plastic tumbler with drink (Annie)
Small paper bag (Jimmy)
     inside: prescription pill bottle with pills
                   vitamin C tablets in bottle
                   Flintstone's Chewable vitamins
                   aspirin bottle in box, seal broken each
                       performance
Aspirins and pills to take (3-4 per performance)
TV Guide magazine
Dishtowel (Grandmother)
Doll (Annie)
Doll clothes (Annie)
Manual typewriter (old, lightweight) (Jimmy)
Typing paper
Cassette tape recorder (Jimmy)
Cassette tapes (approximately 6 blanks with cases) (Jimmy)
Empty Budweiser beer cans (many) (Jimmy)
Unopened Budweiser beer cans (several consumed
    each performance) (Jimmy)

Playing cards (red Bicycle) (Grandmother)
Small baby picture of Wendy (Annie)
Wallet (Annie)
Straw shoulderbag (Annie)
Purse dressing (Annie)
Sunglasses (Annie, Jimmy)
Fan (Annie)
Handkerchief (Jimmy)
Umbrella
Bible
Cigarette holder with cigarette (lit off-stage)

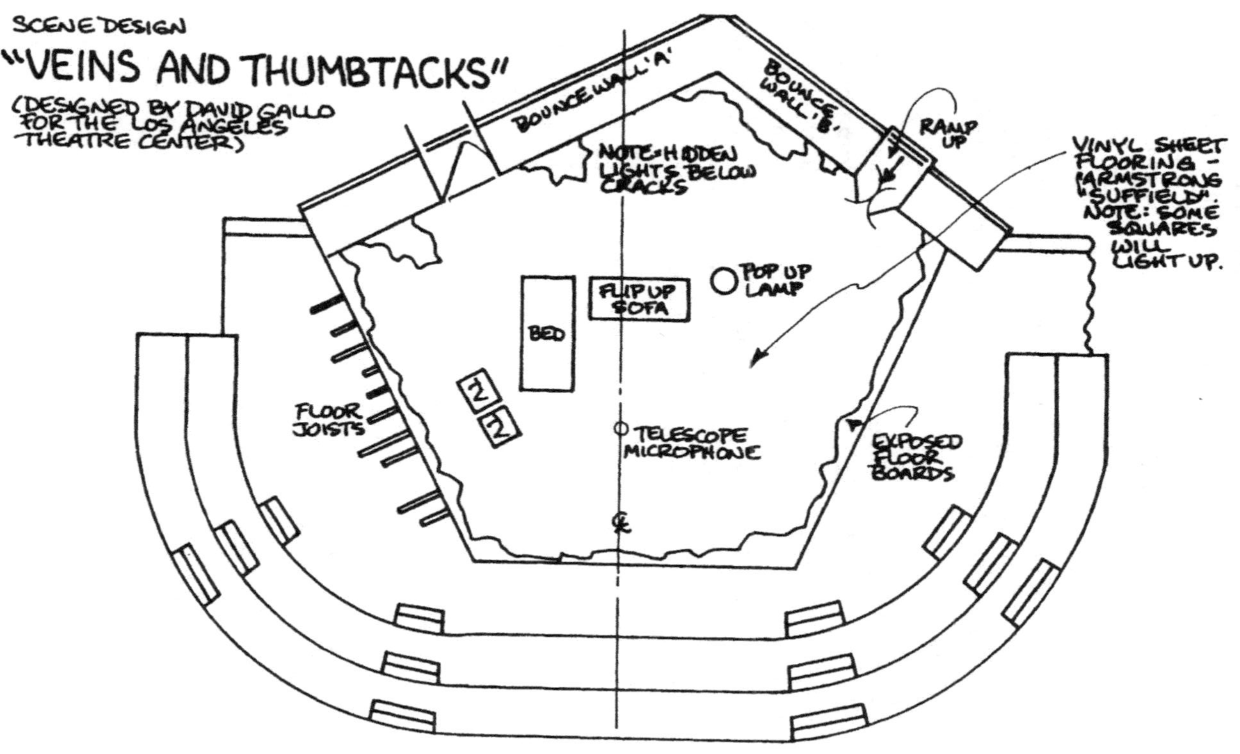

SCENE DESIGN
"VEINS AND THUMBTACKS"
(DESIGNED BY DAVID GALLO
FOR THE LOS ANGELES
THEATRE CENTER)
BOUNCE WALL 'A'
BOUNCE WALL 'B'
RAMP UP
NOTE: HIDDEN LIGHTS BELOW CRACKS
VINYL SHEET FLOORING - ARMSTRONG "SUFFIELD". NOTE: SOME SQUARES WILL LIGHT UP.
POP UP LAMP
FLIP UP SOFA
BED
TV TV
FLOOR JOISTS
TELESCOPE MICROPHONE
EXPOSED FLOOR BOARDS

Note on Songs/Recordings, Images, or Other Production Design Elements

Be advised that Concord Theatricals neither holds the rights to nor grants permission to use any songs, recordings, images, or other design elements mentioned in the play. It is the sole responsibility of the producing theater/organization to obtain permission of the copyright owner(s) for any such use. Additional royalty fees may apply for the right to use copyrighted materials.

For any songs/recordings, images, or other design elements mentioned in the play, works in the public domain may be substituted. It is the producing theater/organization's sole responsibility to ensure the substituted work is indeed in the public domain. Concord Theatricals cannot advise as to whether or not a song/arrangement/recording, image, or other design element is in the public domain.